눈이 즐겁고, 손이 즐겁고, 머리가 즐거운

Early GRAMMAR

English!

2

woongjin
compass

Early GRAMMAR ❷

출판일	1판 2쇄 발행 2015년 8월 14일
지은이	Kate Kim
펴낸이	최희영
책임편집	김소연, 이수미
영문교열	유희숙, 강소영, 김재민, 최나리
디자인	성윤지, 구수연
펴낸곳	(주)컴퍼스미디어
출판신고	1980년 3월 29일 제 406-2007-00046 © ㈜ 웅진씽크빅 2011
주소	서울특별시 서초구 서초2동 1360-31 정진빌딩 3층
전화	(02)3471- 0096
홈페이지	http://www.compasspub.com
ISBN	978-89-6697-770-3

Guide to Early Grammar

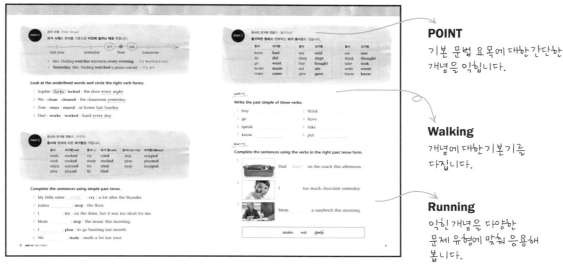

POINT

기본 문법 요목에 대한 간단한
개념을 익힙니다.

Walking

개념에 대한 기본기를
다집니다.

Running

익힌 개념을 다양한
문제 유형에 맞춰 응용해
봅니다.

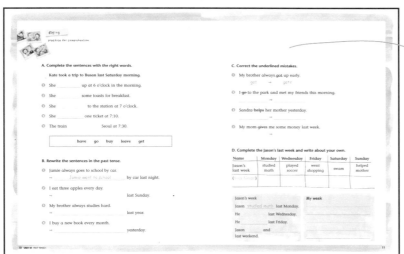

Flying

Writing이 결합된 확장된
형태의 유의미한 activity를
통해, 익힌 개념을 자유롭게
활용합니다.

정답과 해설

정답과 함께
예시 답안을 소개합니다.

Table of
Contents

Unit 1
Past Tense I

일어난 순서에 맞도록 문장을 골라 해당 그림 아래에 쓰세요.

They have three kids.

She **met** Mr. Darling.

They **got** married.

Mrs. Darling **left** music school.

Mrs. Darling left music school.

POiNT 1

과거 시제 (Past Tense)

과거 시제는 현재를 기준으로 **이전에 일어난 때**를 뜻합니다.

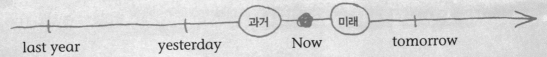

last year   yesterday   Now   tomorrow

- Mrs. Darling **watches** television **every evening**. ➡ 단순 현재 (반복적 일상)
- **Yesterday**, Mrs. Darling **watched** a piano concert. ➡ 단순 과거

Look at the underlined words and circle the right verb forms.

1 Sophie ((locks) / locked) the door every night.

2 We (clean / cleaned) the classroom yesterday.

3 Tom (stays / stayed) at home last Sunday.

4 Dad (works / worked) hard every day.

POiNT 2

동사의 과거형 만들기 (규칙형)

동사의 형태에 따른 **과거형**을 익힙니다.

동사	과거형(-ed)	동사(-y)	과거 형(-ied)	동사(모음+자음)	과거형(자음+ed)
work	work**ed**	cry	cr**ied**	stop	stop**ped**
cook	cook**ed**	study	stud**ied**	plan	plan**ned**
enjoy	enjoy**ed**	try	tr**ied**	mop	mop**ped**
play	play**ed**	fly	fl**ied**		

Complete the sentences using simple past tense.

1 My little sister ___cried___ (**cry**) a lot after the thunder.

2 James _____ (**mop**) the floor.

3 I _____ (**try**) on the dress, but it was too short for me.

4 Mom _____ (**stop**) the music this morning.

5 I _____ (**plan**) to go hunting last month.

6 We _____ (**study**) math a lot last year.

POINT 3 동사의 과거형 만들기 (불규칙형)

불규칙한 형태로 변화하는 **과거 동사**들도 있습니다.

동사	과거형
have	**had**
do	**did**
go	**went**
make	**made**
come	**came**

동사	과거형
say	**said**
sleep	**slept**
buy	**bought**
eat	**ate**
give	**gave**

동사	과거형
see	**saw**
think	**thought**
take	**took**
write	**wrote**
know	**knew**

walking

Write the past simple of these verbs.

1 buy _____   2 think _____

3 go _____   4 have _____

5 speak _____   6 take _____

7 know _____   8 put _____

Running

Complete the sentences using the verbs in the right past tense form.

1  Dad ___slept___ on the couch this afternoon.

2  I _____ too much chocolate yesterday.

3  Mom _____ a sandwich this morning.

| make | eat | ~~sleep~~ |

9

flYing

practice for comprehension

A. Complete the sentences with the right words.

Kate took a trip to Busan last Saturday morning.

❶ She _____ up at 6 o'clock in the morning.

❷ She _____ some toasts for breakfast.

❸ She _____ to the station at 7 o'clock.

❹ She _____ one ticket at 7:10.

❺ The train _____ Seoul at 7:30.

have	go	buy	leave	get

B. Rewrite the sentences in the past tense.

❶ Jamie always goes to school by car.

➡ _____Jamie went to school_____ by car last night.

❷ I eat three apples every day.

➡ _____ last Sunday.

❸ My brother always studies hard.

➡ _____ last year.

❹ I buy a new book every month.

➡ _____ yesterday.

C. Correct the underlined mistakes.

❶ My brother always <u>got</u> up early.

　　　　got　　➡　　　gets

❷ I <u>go</u> to the park and met my friends this morning.

　　　　　　　　➡

❸ Sandra <u>helps</u> her mother yesterday.

　　　　　　➡

❹ My mom <u>gives</u> me some money last week.

　　　　　　➡

D. Complete the Jason's last week and write about your own.

Name	Monday	Wednesday	Friday	Saturday	Sunday
Jason's last week	studied math	played soccer	went shopping	swam	helped mother
(Your Name)					

Jason's week

Jason　studied math　last Monday.

He 　　　　　　　 last Wednesday.

He 　　　　　　　 last Friday.

Jason 　　　　 and 　　　　　　
last weekend.

My week

Unit 2
Past Tense II

다음 대화를 읽고, Sally가 사용한 음식 재료에 동그라미를 하세요.

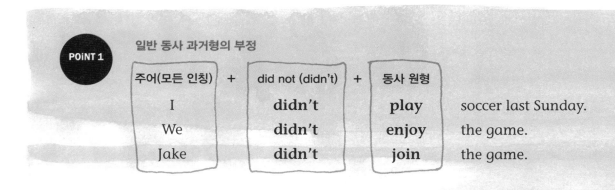

POINT 1 일반 동사 과거형의 부정

주어(모든 인칭)	+	did not (didn't)	+	동사 원형	
I		**didn't**		**play**	soccer last Sunday.
We		**didn't**		**enjoy**	the game.
Jake		**didn't**		**join**	the game.

walk*ing*

Circle the right verb to the picture.

1 It (**rained** / (**didn't rain**)) yesterday.

2 Carol (**made** / **didn't make**) a sandwich.

3 We (**went** / **didn't go**) for a walk.

4 My mother (**bought** / **didn't buy**) roses.

Run*ning*

Complete the sentences with the <u>negative</u> forms.

1 I met Sandy, but I *didn't meet* David.

2 Dad worked on Saturday, but he _____ on Sunday.

3 We went to the park, but we _____ to the museum.

4 Jane had a nice skirt, but she _____ any jacket.

5 My mother studied French at school, but she _____ Spanish.

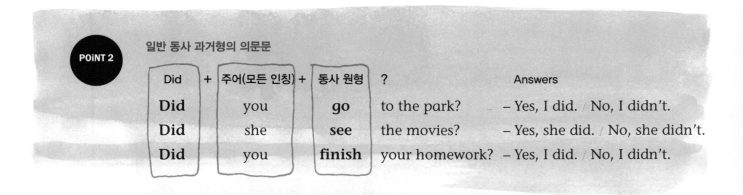

POINT 2 일반 동사 과거형의 의문문

Did	+ 주어(모든 인칭) +	동사 원형	?	Answers
Did	you	**go**	to the park?	– Yes, I did. / No, I didn't.
Did	she	**see**	the movies?	– Yes, she did. / No, she didn't.
Did	you	**finish**	your homework?	– Yes, I did. / No, I didn't.

walking

Complete the questions using simple past tense.

1 The baby cried last night.

___Did___ the baby ___cry___ last night?

2 The students cleaned the classroom.

_____ the students _____ the classroom?

3 The boys had dinner after the game.

_____ the boys _____ dinner after game?

4 Mom stopped the car.

_____ mom _____ the car?

Running

Rewrite the sentences in the correct question form.

1 I watched the film last night. How about you?

➡ ___Did you watch the film?___

2 I had a great holiday. How about you?

➡ _____

3 I finished the homework. How about you?

➡ _____

4 I had a lot of homework last night. How about you?

➡ _____

15

flying

practice for comprehension

A. Read what Peter does every Tuesday. Now, write what he did or didn't do last Tuesday.

On Tuesdays

Peter gets up at 6 o'clock.   Peter eats cereal for breakfast.

Peter studies English at school.   Peter plays soccer after school.

1 Peter ___got up___ at 6 o'clock. He ___didn't get up___ at 5 o'clock.

2 Peter _____ cereal for breakfast. He _____ any bread.

3 Peter _____ English at school. He _____ math.

4 Peter _____ soccer after school. He _____ baseball.

B. Put the verb in the correct forms among positive or negative.

1 Adam went to the camp last month, but it was boring.

In fact, he ___didn't enjoy___ it. (**enjoy**)

2 John was busy yesterday, so he _____ a picnic with his friends.

(**have**)

3 Sam was very tired, so he _____ home last night. (**stay**)

4 It was very cold in the morning, so I _____ the window.

(**close**)

C. Read the text and correct the underlined mistakes.

Last Monday, ❶ Sam loses his key. Sam couldn't go into the house, so ❷ he goes back to school to find the key. Sam's friend Tom went with him. ❸ "Did you looked at your bag carefully?" Tom asked. ❹ "No, I did," Sam said, "I didn't lose it! I just found it in my back pocket!"

❶   loses   ➡   lost

❷   ➡

❸   ➡

❹   ➡

D. Make questions and write about your partner's last year.

Partner's Name :

❶ live in Seoul

Q : Did you live in Seoul last year? ➡ Sam lived in Seoul last year.

❷ play soccer

Q :   ➡

❸ travel abroad

Q :   ➡

❹ study English

Q :   ➡

Unit 3
Future

There **will be** the talent contest next month.
Tina said, "I'll **play** the guitar and sing."
Jake said, "I'll **do** magic tricks."
Dave said, "I'll **tap** dance!"
They **will practice** hard. They **will have** fun.

Jake

Dave

Tina

미래 시제 (Future Tense)

미래에 일어날 일을 표현할 때는 미래 시제인 will (not) + 동사 원형을 사용합니다.

● Every day, I play basketball. ➡ 일상 (단순 현재)

주어	+	will('ll) will not (won't)	+	동사 원형
I		**will** **will not** **(won't)**		**play** **stop**

tomorrow, too. ➡ 앞으로의 일 (미래 시제)
playing it.

Circle the right verb to the picture.

1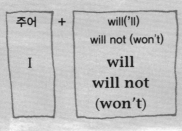

A : What is the weather like tomorrow?
B : It (**rains** / (**will rain**)) tomorrow.

2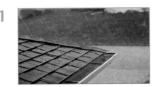

A : What is on the movies next month?
B : *Star Wars* (**shows** / **will show**) soon.

3

A : Where is Sue?
B : She (**is** / **will be**) in Rome next week.

POiNT 2

be going to

미래 시제에 **be(am/are/is) going to + 동사 원형**을 쓰기도 합니다.

주어	+	be (not) going to	+	동사 원형
I		**am going to**		**go**
It		**is going to**		**rain.**

back home.

Circle the right words.

1 My father is at work. He ((**is going to**) / **isn't going to**) be home at 8:00.

2 Take an umbrella. It (**is going to** / **isn't going to**) rain tonight.

3 A : I feel sick.

B : Have some water. You (**are going to** / **aren't going to**) feel better.

4 I want to buy a new car. I (**am going to** / **am not going to**) buy a car next month.

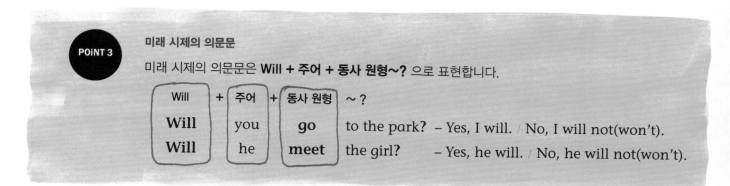

POINT 3

미래 시제의 의문문

미래 시제의 의문문은 **Will + 주어 + 동사 원형~?** 으로 표현합니다.

Will +	주어 +	동사 원형	~ ?	
Will	you	**go**	to the park?	– Yes, I will. / No, I will not(won't).
Will	he	**meet**	the girl?	– Yes, he will. / No, he will not(won't).

Complete the questions about future.

1 I want to be a movie star. ___Will___ I pass the audition next week?

2 I am not married. _____ I meet my future husband this year?

3 My dad will open a flower shop. _____ the shop go well?

4 I jog every morning. _____ I become healthier?

Look at the picture and complete the answer using 'will' or 'will not (won't).'

1   Will she study this evening?

➡ ___Yes___, she ___will___.

2   Will Dave sleep all day?

➡ _____, he _____.

3   Will Ann ride horses on Sunday?

➡ _____, she _____.

flying

practice for comprehension

A. Complete the sentences using 'be going to + verb' in the box.

❶ My hands are dirty. ___I'm going to wash___ them.

❷ I don't want to drive today. _____ to the office.

❸ I am very bored. _____ the movie tonight.

❹ I'm thirsty. _____ some water.

wash   drink   walk   watch

B. Make questions and answers using 'will/won't + verb.'

❶

have

Q : __Will__ she __have__ a salad?

A : __No__ , she __won't have__ a salad.

She __will have__ some steak.

❷

travel

Q : _____ they _____ in China next summer?

A : _____ , they _____ in China.

They _____ in France.

❸

study

Q : _____ he _____ at 3 o'clock tomorrow?

A : _____ , he _____ at 3 o'clock.

He _____ at 5 o'clock.

C. Read the text and correct the underlined mistakes.

My brother Jack is brave. ❶ He will ~~is~~ a policeman. ❷ He will ~~helping~~ many people. I am not brave, but I am very smart. ❸ I will ~~am~~ a scientist. ❹ I will ~~invented~~ new robots. The robots will help many people.

❶ _____is_____ ➡ _____be_____

❷ _____ ➡ _____

❸ _____ ➡ _____

❹ _____ ➡ _____

D. Amy is travelling in Korea. Complete the sentence with the future tense using the words given.

Amy left Seoul yesterday.

Tomorrow, she ____will be____ in Daejeon. (**be**)

She _____ her friends there. (**meet**)

Next week, Amy _____ to Busan. (**go**)

She _____ by the KTX train. (**travel**)

After that, she _____ to Jeju. (**go**)

At the end of her trip, she _____ very tired. (**be**)

Unit 4

Present Progressive

● 다음 그림을 보고, 문장의 동사에 동그라미를 하고 그림과 내용이 맞으면 True, 틀리면 False에 체크하세요.

1 Dona **is wearing** a check skirt.　　　　True　　　False

2 Dona's mom **is carrying** a cake.　　　　True　　　False

3 The children **are having** fun at the party.　　True　　　False

Dona

Sandy

Kate

Dona's dad

POiNT 1

현재 진행 시제 (Present Progressive)

말하고 있는 **지금 일어나고 있는 일**은 현재 진행형(be + V-ing)으로 표현합니다.

- I play the guitar every day. ➡ 이상적인 일 (단순 현재)

주어	+	be동사 (not)	+	V-ing
I		**am not**		**playing**
I		**am**		**watching**

the guitar **now**. ➡ 지금 하는 일(현재 진행)

TV.

Circle the right verb form to the picture.

1
Jack (**paints** / is painting) every day.
But, he (doesn't paint / **isn't painting**) now.
He is playing the guitar.

Jake - a painter

2
Lisa and Sam (cook / are cooking) every day.
But, they (don't cook / aren't cooking) now.
They are running.

Lisa & Sam - cooks

POiNT 2

현재 진행형 만들기

V-ing 형태는 다음의 원칙을 따릅니다.

기본형	'-e'로 끝나는 동사	'모음+자음'으로 끝나는 동사
do – do**ing**	make – mak**ing**	run – run**ning**
go – go**ing**	have – hav**ing**	stop – stop**ping**
call – call**ing**	write – writ**ing**	sit – sit**ting**

Write the present progressive form of these verbs.

1 dance _____   2 think _____

3 go _____   4 have _____

5 speak _____   6 take _____

7 know _____   8 put _____

9 meet _____   10 swim _____

현재 진행형 의문문

현재 진행형의 의문형은 '**be + 주어 + V-ing ?**' 형태로 구성됩니다.

be 동사	+	주어	+	V-ing	? Answers
Am		I		**talking**	fast? – Yes, you are. / No, you aren't.
Are		you/we/they		**listening**	now? – Yes, I am. / No, I'm not.
Is		he/she/it		**doing**	well? – Yes, he is. / No, he isn't.

walking

Write questions using present progressive.

1 You are learning science. ⇒ Are you learning science?

2 She is drawing a bird. ⇒ _____

3 David is running very fast. ⇒ _____

4 We are listening to music. ⇒ _____

Running

Complete the sentences using the verbs given.

1 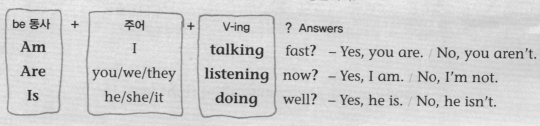 ___Is___ Dad ___sleeping___ on the couch? (**sleep**)
   – Yes, he is.

2 _____ Mom _____ dishes? (**wash**)
   – _____

3 _____ you _____ some salad? (**eat**)
   – _____

4 _____ you _____ in the garden? (**work**)
   – _____

flying

practice for comprehension

A. Complete the sentences in the right verb forms.

1

Jimmy _isn't_ _sitting_ on a chair. (**sit**)

2

They _____ _____ baseball. (**play**)

3

Sarah _____ _____ in the park. (**walk**)

4

He _____ _____ orange juice. (**drink**)

B. Unscramble the words.

1 Emma / her face / washing / is

➡ _____

2 having / the teachers / are / a tea time

➡ _____

3 is / he / his mother / listening to / not

➡ _____

4 strawberry candies / selling / they / are

➡ _____

C. Underline the mistakes, and rewrite the full sentence.

1 Jane and I are ~~walked~~ to school now.

➡ *Jane and I are walking to school now.*

2 Anna doesn't speaking on the phone.

➡ _____

3 Look at Sandra! She speaks Japanese now.

➡ _____

4 My little brother is have some chicken in the shop.

➡ _____

D. What are the people doing in the picture? Write the sentences about the people in the picture.

1 (play table tennis)

➡ *He is playing table tennis.*

2 (drink water)

➡ _____

3 (run on the treadmill)

➡ _____

4 (do push-ups)

➡ _____

Unit 5
Modal Verbs

다음 문장의 동사에 동그라미를 하고, Jake의 캠프 생활을 묘사한
문장과 그림을 연결해 보세요.

1 He can ride a horse or climb the rock. ( )

2 He eats some breakfast.

3 He has to get up early
   in the morning.

4 He has to make his bed.

5 He has to run 2 kilometers.

POiNT 1

능력, 가능성의 can

'~할 수 있다'라는 의미에는 **can + 동사 원형**을 씁니다.

〈평서문〉 | 〈의문문〉
주어 + (**can** / **can't**) + 동사 원형 | (**Can** / **Can't**) + 주어 + 동사 원형 ?

A : **Can** you **play** the violin?
B : Yes, I **can** play the violin.

Circle the right words to the picture.

1  Judy (**can** / **can't**) fly a kite.

2  Chris (**can** / **can't**) play soccer.

3  I (**can** / **can't**) do my homework.

4  Turtles (**can** / **can't**) run fast.

POiNT 2

허가, 승낙의 can

허가나 **승낙**을 받을 때에도 **can + 동사 원형**을 사용합니다.

A : **Can** you **open** the door, please? | A : **Can** I **turn** on the TV?
B : Sure. | B : No, you **can't**.

Complete sentence using 'can' or 'can't.'

1 I didn't have a phone.   _Can_   I use your phone?

2 A : Sally, you _____ have sweet dissert after dinner.

  B : Thanks, mom. I want to have some chocolate cake.

3 A : Mom, can I play outside?

  B : It's too late. You _____ go outside.

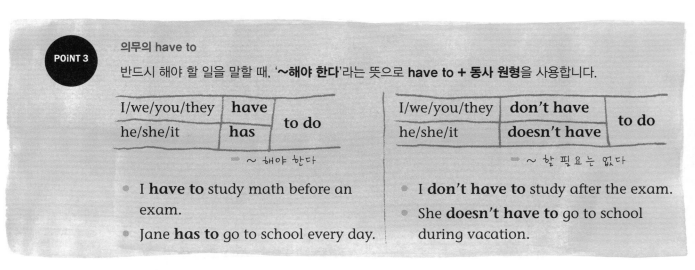

POINT 3

의무의 have to

반드시 해야 할 일을 말할 때, '∼해야 한다'라는 뜻으로 **have to + 동사 원형**을 사용합니다.

| I/we/you/they | **have** | **to do** |
| he/she/it | **has** | |

∼ 해야 한다

* I **have to** study math before an exam.
* Jane **has to** go to school every day.

| I/we/you/they | **don't have** | **to do** |
| he/she/it | **doesn't have** | |

∼ 할 필요는 없다

* I **don't have to** study after the exam.
* She **doesn't have to** go to school during vacation.

walking

Circle the right words.

1 I (**have to**/ **has to**) go to school.

2 Sarah (**don't have to** / **doesn't have to**) go to school today.

3 Peter (**have to** / **doesn't have to**) study now.

4 We (**have to** / **has to**) wait for the teacher.

Running

Complete the sentences using 'have/has to + verb' from the box.

1 I'm late for school. I _____have to take_____ a taxi.

2 Jake's room is a mess. He _____ the room.

3 My friends are hungry. They _____ something.

4 We are very tired. We _____ to bed early.

| take | eat | go | clean |

fly**ing**

practice for comprehension

A. Make questions and write <u>your own answers</u>. Use 'can + verb.'

1 swim

Q : _Can you swim?_

My Answer : _I can swim._

2 ski

Q : _____

My Answer : _____

3 ride a bike

Q : _____

My Answer : _____

4 drive a car

Q : _____

My Answer : _____

B. Complete the sentences. Use 'have to' or 'don't have to' + verb.

1 My room is clean. I _don't have to clean_ the room.

2 It's Sunday. I _____ to school today.

3 I am late. I _____ now.

4 My eyes are not good. I _____ glasses.

| clean | wear | leave | go |

C. Underline the mistakes, and rewrite the correct sentence.

❶ Can you help me tomorrow? – Yes, I ~~will~~ can help you tomorrow.

➡ _Yes, I can help you tomorrow._

❷ Bill can't go to the party. He have to work.

➡ _____

❸ My father starts work at 7 o'clock. He can have to get up at 6 o'clock.

➡ _____

D. Explain the safety signs using 'can' or 'have to.'

Safety Signs

❶ You _____can_____ enter.

❷ You _____ slow down when you are driving.

❸ You _____ park your bicycle.

❹ Do not run. You _____ walk.

Unit 6
Linking Verbs

다음 대화에서 Amy가 할 말로 적당한 것은 무엇일까요?

1 I ate some fruits. They **tasted sweet**.

2 I drank some milk in the fridge. It **smelled bad**.

3 I slept very well. I **feel great**.

연결 동사 (Linking Verb)

형용사가 주어를 설명하도록 돕는 동사를 **연결 동사**(Linking Verb)라고 합니다.

- This is a nice garden. ➡ 형용사의 역할 : 명사 수식(형용사+명사)

주어	+	연결 동사	+	형용사
The flowers		**smell**		**sweet**.
They		**look**		**beautiful**.

➡ 형용사의 역할 : 주어를 설명(동사+형용사)

연결 동사 : be, sound, taste, look, smell, feel

walking

Circle the right linking verbs.

1 Tom ((**looks**) / **sounds**) handsome.

2 The violin (**looks** / **sounds**) great.

3 This ice cream (**sounds** / **tastes**) sweet.

4 The garbage (**has** / **smells**) terrible.

Running

Put the right adjectives into the columns from the box. You can use the adjectives more than once.

1 The music sounds	2 The soup tastes	3 The flower smells	4 The pet feels	5 The boy looks ....
quiet, beautiful				

> delicious   salty   small   big   ~~quiet~~   soft
> terrible   hard   ~~beautiful~~   ugly

연결 동사 + 형용사

연결 동사는 형용사와 함께 사용하며, **일반 동사는 부사와** 함께 사용됩니다.

| 주어 | + | 연결 동사 | + | 형용사 |
| Sarah | | **is** | | **quiet.** |

(~~quietly~~) → 형용사 : 주어 설명

| 주어 | + | 일반 동사 | + | 부사 |
| She | | **speaks** | | **quietly.** |

(~~quiet~~) → 부사 : 동사 수식

walking

Circle the right words.

1 The meat smelled ((bad) / **badly**).

2 Jim drives (**slow** / **slowly**).

3 The cake looks (**sweet** / **sweetly**).

4 The girl plays (**happy** / **happily**).

Running

Complete the sentences using the verbs from the box.

1 The coffee _smells_ good.

2 The boy doesn't speak at all.
He _____ badly.

3 It is very windy. I _____ cold.

4 The music band is very popular.
They _____ nicely.

behave	**feel**	**play**	~~**smell**~~

fl**y**ing

practice for comprehension

A. Unscramble the words.

① sour / tastes / the / orange / big

➡ _____The big orange tastes sour._____

② felt / the / cloth / soft / yellow

➡ _____

③ the sky / black / was

➡ _____

④ my dad / fast / drives / very

➡ _____

B. Complete the sentences using one of the words given.

① 그 쇼가 아주 흥미롭게 들린다. (**interesting** / **interestingly**)

➡ That show sounds very _____interesting_____ .

② 우리 선생님은 따뜻하게 말씀하신다. (**warm** / **warmly**)

➡ My teacher speaks _____ .

③ 이 생선은 나쁜 냄새가 난다. (**bad** / **badly**)

➡ This fish smells _____ .

④ 무슨 일이야? 너 심각하게 보인다. (**serious** / **seriously**)

➡ What's wrong? You look _____ .

C. Underline the mistakes and rewrite the full sentence.

1 Does it taste ~~badly~~?

➡ Does it taste bad?

2 The kids look sadly.

➡ _____

3 The farmers work slow.

➡ _____

4 This wine tastes wonderfully.

➡ _____

D. Read the story and complete the summary using the words in the story.

A Shopping Day

  Yesterday, my friend and I went to the shopping mall. There was a band at the mall. They played rock music. It sounded great. We ate in the noodle soup restaurant. The noodle tasted wonderful. We went to the pet store. There was a snake. It looked scary. Then, we went to the toy store. I bought a pig doll for my sister. It felt soft.

➡ There was a band at the mall. The music ____sounded great____ .
  We ate the noodle soup. It _____ .
  We went to the pet store. The snake _____ .
  I bought a pig doll. It _____ .

Unit 7
Quantifiers

Kevin	Tom	David
some rice a little honey some water		

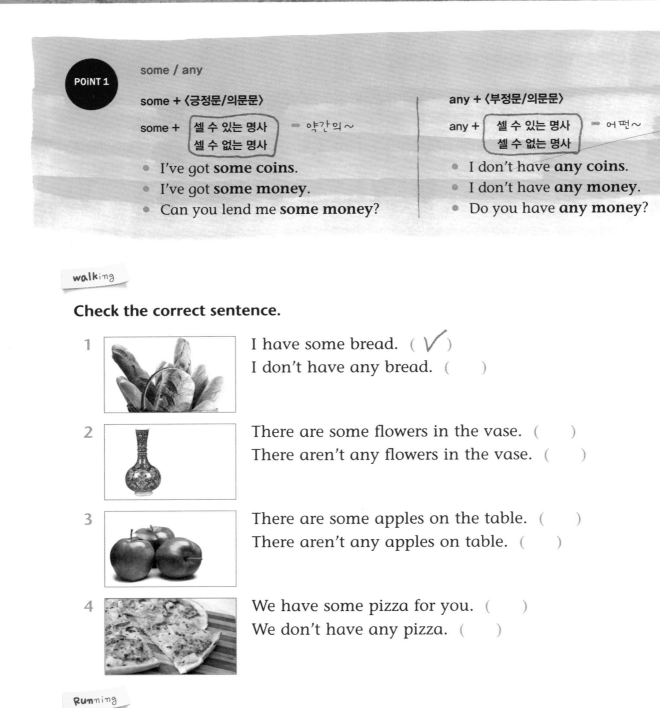

POINT 1

some / any

some + 〈긍정문/의문문〉

some + [셀 수 있는 명사 / 셀 수 없는 명사] ➡ 약간의~

- I've got **some coins**.
- I've got **some money**.
- Can you lend me **some money**?

any + 〈부정문/의문문〉

any + [셀 수 있는 명사 / 셀 수 없는 명사] ➡ 어떤~

- I don't have **any coins**.
- I don't have **any money**.
- Do you have **any money**?

walking

Check the correct sentence.

1   I have some bread. (✓)
    I don't have any bread. (   )

2   There are some flowers in the vase. (   )
    There aren't any flowers in the vase. (   )

3   There are some apples on the table. (   )
    There aren't any apples on table. (   )

4   We have some pizza for you. (   )
    We don't have any pizza. (   )

Running

Write 'some or any.'

1   I bought ___some___ magazines and ___some___ cookies

2   I am thirsty. I want to drink _____ water.

3   There aren't _____ students in the room.

4   I need _____ cheese, but I don't need _____ bread.

POiNT 2

a lot of / many / much

'많은' 이라는 의미의 **a lot of, many, much**도 그 용법이 다릅니다.

a lot of + | 셀 수 있는 명사
             셀 수 없는 명사

many + | 셀 수 있는 명사

much + | 셀 수 없는 명사

a lot of money (많은 돈)
a lot of students (많은 학생들)

not **much** money (많지 않은 돈)
not **many** students (많지 않은 학생들)

Circle the right words.

1 Did you buy (**many** / **much**) juice?

2 Do you read (**many** / **much**) books?

3 I don't have (**many** / **much**) time.

4 There aren't (**many** / **much**) hotels in my city.

5 I didn't eat (**many** / **much**) food at dinner. I'm hungry.

6 I need (**many** / **much**) toys for the children.

POiNT 3

a little / a few

'약간의 / 몇몇의' 라는 의미의 **a little**과 **a few**의 용법을 알아둡니다.

(a) little + | 셀 수 없는 명사

(a) few + | 셀 수 있는 명사(복수형)

a little water
a little air
a little food

a few boys
a few books
a few people

a little : 조금 있는 / little : 거의 없는

a few : 조금 있는 / few : 거의 없는

Circle the right words.

1 (**a little** / **a few**) boxes

2 (**a little** / **a few**) money

3 (**a little** / **a few**) rain

4 (**a little** / **a few**) countries

5 (**a little** / **a few**) help

6 (**a little** / **a few**) bottles

fly_ing_

practice for comprehension

A. Write 'some' or 'any' with one of words in the box.

❶ I want to take a shower. Do you have _any towel_ ?

❷ There are _____ in my mother's garden.

❸ I didn't have money, so I didn't buy _____ in the bakery.

bread   towel   flowers

B. Write 'much' or 'many' with one of words in the box.

❶ I am hungry because I didn't eat _much food_ .

❷ I like reading, but I don't have _____ .

❸ There aren't _____ in this school. It is quiet.

students   food   books

C. Write 'a little' or 'a few' with one of words in the box.

❶ I want to buy a new car, but I only have _a little money_ .

❷ I'm not full because I had _____ for breakfast.

❸ I missed the train. It left _____ ago.

minutes   bread   money

D. Complete the sentences using the right words in the box.

❶ 나는 식료품점에서 약간의 채소를 사고 싶다.

➡ I want to buy ___some___ vegetables at the grocery.

❷ 서둘러. 시간이 많지 않아!

➡ Hurry. You don't have _____ time!

❸ 너랑 놀 수가 없다. 집안일을 몇 가지 해야 해.

➡ I can't play with you. I have to do _____ chores.

❹ 우리 부모님은 어떤 애완동물도 없다.

➡ My parents don't have _____ pets.

some	any	much	many	a few

E. Imagine you are going camping for a week. Choose 4 things that you need. Use 'many/much/a few/a little/a lot of.'

Things I need for camping
• a little water or a lot of water
• _____
• _____
• _____

Unit 8
Frequency Adverb

● 위의 대화를 읽고, 질문에 답하세요.

1 Who eats hamburgers and who doesn't?

➡ _____ **often eats** hamburgers but _____ **never eats** them.

2 What does Sandra usually eat?

➡ She **usually eats** _____.

POiNT 1

부사 (Adverb)

부사는 형용사 혹은 동사를 자세히 설명해 주는 역할을 합니다.

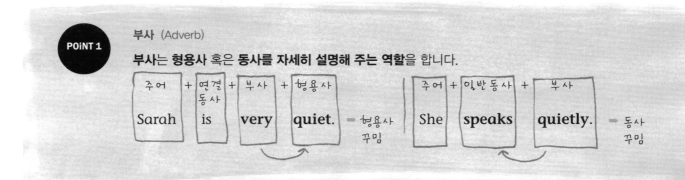

Circle adverbs in the sentences.

1 It is raining (heavily.)

2 I didn't sleep well.

3 I open the door carefully.

4 The man sings loudly.

5 She can run very fast.

6 Ben walks slowly.

7 Jane is studying hard.

POiNT 2

빈도 부사 (Frequency Adverb)

빈도 부사는 어떤 일이 얼마나 자주 일어나는지를 설명하는 부사입니다.

- Tom is **usually** busy.
  He **sometimes** helps his mother.

- Tim is **always** busy.
  He **never** helps his mother.

always ⇒ usually ⇒ often ⇒ sometimes ⇒ rarely ⇒ never
100%   0%

Circle the right frequency adverb about <u>yourself</u>.

1 I am (**never** / **often** / **always**) late for school.

2 I (**never** / **rarely** / **sometimes**) help my mom.

3 My dad (**never** / **often** / **sometimes**) takes out the garbage.

4 My dad (**never** / **often** / **sometimes**) cooks.

5 My mother (**never** / **sometimes** / **always**) helps my homework.

6 My father (**never** / **often** / **always**) tells me what to do.

POINT 3

빈도 부사의 어순

빈도 부사의 어순은 다음과 같습니다.

- Mom **always drinks** coffee in the morning. ➡ 일반동사 앞
- I **am always** tired in the morning. ➡ be 동사 뒤
- We **don't always like** morning. ➡ 조동사와 일반 동사 사이

---

walking

Check the place for the frequency adverb and write it.

1 Sally is ✓ nice to her friends. (**always**)
➡ ~~Sally is always nice to her friends.~~

2 I finish my homework in the morning. (**usually**)
➡ _____

3 Mike doesn't work on weekends. (**always**)
➡ _____

4 I will forget your help. (**never**)
➡ _____

Running

Look at answers in the box and rewrite the sentence about Sam.

1 Does Sam exercise?   (✓) always   ( ) sometimes   ( ) never
Sam exercises.   ➡ ~~Sam always exercises.~~

2 Does Sam study hard?   ( ) always   ( ) sometimes   (✓) never
Sam studies hard.   ➡ _____

3 Is Sam busy?   ( ) always   (✓) sometimes   ( ) never
Sam is busy.   ➡ _____

4 Does Sam go fishing?   (✓) always   ( ) sometimes   ( ) never
Sam goes fishing.   ➡ _____

flYing

practice for comprehension

A. Rewrite the sentences with the frequency adverbs.

❶ Kevin talks a lot. (**always**)

➥ _____ Kevin always talks a lot. _____

❷ I can remember his birthday. (**never**)

➥ _____

❸ I don't eat fast food. (**often**)

➥ _____

❹ The train isn't late. (**usually**)

➥ _____

B. Complete the sentence in the right order.

❶ 엄마는 보통은 커피에 우유를 타 드신다. (**take / usually**)

➥ Mom _____ usually takes _____ milk in coffee.

❷ 나는 그 여행을 결코 잊을 수가 없어. (**can / forget / never**)

➥ I _____ the trip.

❸ LA에서는 비가 자주 오지 않는다. (**often / doesn't / rain**)

➥ It _____ in LA.

❹ 그들은 주말에 절대 집에 있지 않는다. (**never / are / at home**)

➥ They _____ on weekend.

C. Read the text and correct and rewrite the story.

Sunday ~~never~~ is a quiet day for our family. We have to help mother. Outside, my little brother Chris cleans the windows. He works ~~always~~ hard. In the garden, Dad ~~usually~~ is busy cutting grass. I don't like house chores, but I ~~always must~~ help mom and dad.

➡ _____

_____

_____

_____

D. Think about what chores/activities you do on Sunday. Write about what your families do on Sunday.

Who?	How often?	What chores?
Dad	always	cleans the house

My dad always cleans the house on Sundays.

_____

_____

Unit 9
Comparative & Superlative

다음 그림을 보고 각 문장이 맞으면 True, 틀리면 False에 동그라미를 하세요.

1 Asian elephants are **heavier than** African elephants.   True   False

2 Asian elephants are **shorter than** African elephants.   True   False

3 The tusks of African elephants are **bigger**.   True   False

4 The skin of African elephants is **smoother**.   True   False

Asian Elephant

Weight : 3~4 tons
Height : 2~3 meters
Tusks : small
Skin : smooth

Weight : 6~7 tons
Height : 3~4 meters
Tusks : big
Skin : tough

African Elephant

POiNT 1

비교급 (Comparative)

두 가지를 비교하는 경우 비교급 표현을 사용합니다.

short word ~ -er	word+y ~ -ier	long word ~ more ~
old – old**er**	easy – eas**ier**	beautiful – **more** beautiful
small – small**er**	heavy – heav**ier**	famous – **more** famous
big – big**ger**	early – earl**ier**	expensive – **more** expensive
hot – hot**ter**	pretty – prett**ier**	careful – **more** careful

불규칙 : good (well) – **better**   bad (badly) – **worse**

Look at the picture and write the comparative.

1
slow   *slower*

2
fast _____

3
early _____

4
high _____

5
happy _____

6
hot _____

POiNT 2

비교급 + than

비교급 뒤에 오는 **than** 은 '**~보다**'라는 의미를 표현합니다.

- I'm **faster than** her.
- The hotel is **more expensive than** the guest house.

Complete the sentences using 'comparative + than.'

1 My painting is _better_ _than_ yours. (**good**)

2 The English test was _____ the math test. (**easy**)

3 My dad is _____ my mother. (**young**)

4 Roses are _____ any other flowers. (**beautiful**)

최상급 (Superlative)

세가지 이상을 비교할 때는 **최상급**이 사용됩니다.

short word — -est	word+y — -iest	long word — the most ~
old – old**est**	easy – eas**iest**	beautiful – **the most** beautiful
small – small**est**	heavy – heav**iest**	famous – **the most** famous
big – big**gest**	early – earl**iest**	expensive – **the most** expensive
hot – hot**test**	pretty – prett**iest**	careful – **the most** careful

불규칙 : good (well) – better – **best**   bad (badly) – worse – **worst**

walking

Look at the picture and write the superlative.

1 slow / fast

the slowest   the fastest

2 young / old

3 low / high

4 cheap / expensive

Running

Write the correct comparative and superlative forms.

1 My dog is <u>smarter</u> than yours, but Carol's dog is <u>the smartest</u>. (**smart**)

2 Kevin's work is _____ than Alex, but Suzan's work is _____.

(**good**)

3 It is _____ than yesterday, but last Monday was _____.

(**cold**)

4 I study _____ than Sam, but Rose studies _____. (**hard**)

fl**y**ing

practice for comprehension

A. Look at the pictures and complete the sentences.

1 The goose's egg is ___bigger than___ the hen's egg.
The ostrich's egg is ___the biggest___ of all. (**big**)

2 Dad is _____ me. Grandfather is
_____ of all. (**old**)

3 I am _____ my little sister. My big
brother is _____ of all. (**tall**)

4 The shoes are _____ the shirt.
The hat is _____ of all. (**cheap**)

B. Write your own sentences using the words given.

1 Mt. Everest / Mt. Fuji (**high**)

➡ ___Mt. Everest is higher than Mt. Fuji.___

2 The sun / The moon (**hot**)

➡ _____

3 A horse / A sheep (**slow**)

➡ _____

4 An elephant's ear / A rabbit's ear (**big**)

➡ _____

C. Underline the mistakes, and rewrite the correct sentence.

➊ African elephants are ~~more heavy~~ than Asian elephants.

➡ _African elephants are heavier than Asian elephants._

➋ Driving a car is more fast than riding a bike.

➡ _____

➌ My dress isn't very pretty. Yours is more pretty.

➡ _____

➍ Sahara is a dry place than Seoul.

➡ _____

D. Compare the panda and the polar bear. Write your own ideas about how they are different using the words given.

The panda

lives in the Arctic	lives in China
friendlier cuter	faster bigger

The polar bear

_____

_____

_____

_____

Unit 10
Gerund

다음 그림을 보고 두 사람의 대화를 완성하세요.

John : _Riding a skateboard_ is my favorite sport.
I don't enjoy _____.

Lisa : I don't enjoy _____.
My favorite activity is _____.

going camping   swimming
~~riding a skateboard~~   cooking food

동명사 (Gerunds) — **명사 역할**

동명사는 **명사 역할**을 하며, **동사-ing** 형태입니다.
문장의 **주어**, **목적어**, **보어**로 사용됩니다.

- **Jogging** is fun. ➡ 주어
- My hobby is **jogging**. ➡ 보어
- I like **playing** sports. ➡ 목적어

walking

Match to the right picture and circle the gerund.

1 My father's hobby is (taking) pictures.

2 Eating candies is bad for your teeth.

3 My sister likes climbing the mountains.

4 My grandmother enjoys knitting.

ⓐ

ⓑ

ⓒ

ⓓ

Running

Circle the gerunds and check in the right box. Translate the sentence into Korean.

	주어	목적어	보어

1 I love (dancing).
➡ 나는 춤 추는 것을 매우 좋아한다.   ✓ (목적어)

2 Ice skating is very difficult.
➡ 아이스 스케이트 타는 것은 아주 어렵다.

3 Cooking is fun.
➡ 요리하는 것은 재미있다.

4 My hobby is collecting old coins.
➡ 나의 취미는 오래된 동전을 모으는 것이다.

동명사 목적어

동명사만을 목적어로 취하는 동사들을 알아둡니다.

| enjoy, stop, finish, keep, mind | + | V-ing (동명사 목적어) ~~to+V or 동사 원형~~ |

- Sam and Jane **enjoy watching** cartoons on TV.
- They didn't **finish watching** it until eleven.
- Their mother **kept telling** them to go to sleep.

walking

Underline the verb and circle the right object.

1 Would you <u>mind</u> ((closing) / close) the window?

2 Maria enjoys (**playing** / **play**) golf.

3 Mom kept (**telling** / **tell**) me what to do.

4 Lisa finished (**making** / **make**) model planes.

5 Dad stopped (**smoking** / **smoke**) last year.

Running

Complete the sentence with the right verb form.

1 Please stop ___playing___ the piano at night. (**play**)

2 Did you finish _____ your homework? (**do**)

3 Do you mind _____ your phone? (**use**)

4 They enjoyed _____ the film. (**watch**)

5 We kept _____ at the pool this morning. (**swim**)

6 Tom needs to stop _____ fast. (**drive**)

fl**y**ing

practice for comprehension

A. Choose the right verb from the box to the picture.

1 Sam couldn't _finish_ doing his homework until midnight.

2 Kevin and I _____ hiking. We hike every weekend.

3 Do you _____ opening the door? This room is very warm.

4 The room was very messy. He had to _____ cleaning the room.

keep	mind	enjoy	~~finish~~

B. Complete the sentence using the words given.

1 우표 모으는 것은 매우 어렵다. (**collect stamps**)

➡ _Collecting stamps_ is very difficult.

2 내가 제일 좋아하는 취미는 한국 음식을 요리하는 것이다. (**cook Korean food**)

➡ My favorite hobby is _____ .

3 도시에 사는 것은 매우 바쁘다. (**live in the city**)

➡ _____ is very busy.

4 Jason은 다른 사람 돕는 것을 즐긴다. (**help other people**)

➡ Jason enjoys _____ .

C. Correct the underlined mistakes, and rewrite the sentence.

❶ I don't mind ~~to stay~~ home on weekends.

⟹   I don't mind staying home on weekends.

❷ ~~Drive~~ is faster than taking a bus.

⟹ _____

❸ My grandmom enjoys ~~to~~ getting up early in the morning.

⟹ _____

❹ ~~Eat~~ fast food is not good for your health.

⟹ _____

D. Choose three favorite activities or things and write them in the chart.
Write about your favorite activities below.

Rona's Favorite	What?	My Favorite	What?
hobby	read stories		
sport	play soccer		
food	eat pizza		

Rona's favorite hobby is _reading_
stories .

She also enjoys _playing soccer_ .

Rona loves _eating pizza_ , too.

My favorite _____ is
_____ .

I also enjoy _____ .

I love _____ , too.

Unit 11
Infinitive

위의 대화를 읽고, 질문에 답하세요.

1 What does Kevin want to become in the future?
→ He wants _____ a teacher.

2 What does Sam like doing?
→ He likes _____ animals.

POiNT 1

to 부정사 (To–Infinitive) **– 명사 역할**

to + 동사 원형을 **to 부정사**라고 하며, 문장에서 **명사**의 역할을 합니다.

- What do you want **to do** this weekend?
  – I want **to go** shopping.

➡ want의 목적어 (명사) 역할

to 부정사만을 목적어로 취하는 **동사**들이 있습니다.

| want, plan, decide, hope, need, learn, try
would like('d like) / would love('d love) | + | to V (to 부정사 목적어)
~~V-ing or 동사 원형~~ |

Underline the verb and circle its object. Then, translate the sentence into Korean.

1 I <u>want</u> (to join) the club.
➡ 나는 그 클럽에 가입하기를 바란다.

2 Maria learns to play tennis.
➡ Maria는 테니스 하는 것을 배운다.

3 Mom decided to buy a new computer.
➡ 엄마는 새 컴퓨터를 사기로 결정했다.

4 It's late. We need to go home.
➡ 늦었어. 우리는 집에 가야 해.

5 I hope to go abroad next year.
➡ 나는 내년에 해외에 나가기를 바란다.

POiNT 2

to 부정사와 동명사

to 부정사와 동명사를 모두 목적어로 갖는 **동사**들도 있습니다.

| like, love, start,
prefer, hate, begin | + | V-ing / to 부정사 |

- Do you **like visiting** the zoo? / Do you **like to visit** the zoo?

Circle all the correct words.

1 He likes (**play** / (**to play**) / (**playing**)) basketball.

2 John prefers (**study** / **to study** / **studying**) math.

3 Alex hopes (**go** / **to go** / **going**) to Brazil next summer.

4 Jerry starts (**work** / **to work** / **working**) in the bakery.

5 Jason begin (**watch** / **to watch** / **watching**) the video.

6 Mom loves (**walk** / **to walk** / **walking**) in the forest.

POINT 3

to 부정사 - 형용사 역할

to 부정사가 **형용사의 역할**을 할 때는, 앞에 나오는 **명사를 꾸며**줍니다.

- Joan bought some **juice to drink**. ⟹ to drink : juice를 수식 (마실 주스)

She also bought a **book to read**. ⟹ to read : book을 수식 (읽을 책)

Circle the infinitives and check in the right box. Translate the sentence into Korean.

1 We have a lot of snacks (to eat.)

형용사   명사

    ✓

⟹   우리는 먹을 간식이 많이 있다.

2 I don't have a key to open the door.

⟹ 나는 문을 열 열쇠가 없다.

3 Jane hopes to meet her cousin.

⟹ Jane은 그녀의 사촌을 만나기를 바란다.

POINT 4

to 부정사 - 부사 역할

to 부정사가 **부사의 역할**을 할 때는, '**~하기 위해서**'라는 어떤 일의 **목적**을 설명하는데 사용됩니다.

- I went to the cinema **to watch** the film. ⟹ 영화를 보기 위해

I watch the film **to have** fun. ⟹ 재미있기 위해

Look at the pictures and circle the right words.

1

Why did you stay up last night?
– I stayed up ((to do my homework)/ to go out with friends).

2

Why did Anne get up early?
– She got up early (to jog / to stay home).

3

Why did you go to the mall?
– I went to the mall (to buy a shirt / to meet a friend).

flying

practice for comprehension

A. Put the words in the right forms.

1 I learnt ___to ski___ five years ago. (**ski**)

2 What do you plan _____ tonight? (**do**)
– I'd like _____ my friend's house. (**visit**)

3 Did you finish _____ your homework? (**do**)
– No, but I decided _____ the film. (**watch**)

4 Where is Anna? I need _____ a question. (**ask**)
– Sorry. She doesn't want _____ anyone. (**meet**)

B. Look at the pictures and complete the sentence using the words in the box.

1  I need a saucepan ___to boil___ water.

2  Jack bought an oven _____ a pie.

3  We have a knife _____ the meat.

4  I brought a chair _____.

| boil   cut   bake   sit on |

C. Correct the underlined mistakes, and rewrite the sentence.

❶ Jake decided becoming a doctor.

➡ Jake decided to become a doctor.

❷ I want seeing you soon.

➡

❸ We hope visit your country next summer.

➡

❹ Would you like go to the park?

➡

D. Read the text and complete the summary using 'to-V.'

Sam decided to become a doctor. He will go to Africa to help children.
Lisa works hard to become a dancer. She wants to be very famous.
Matt hopes to teach poor children. He studies hard to become a teacher.
Joe began painting 4 years ago. He plans to go to Paris to study art.

- Sam decided _____ a doctor to help African children. (**become**)

- Lisa works hard _____ a famous dancer. (**become**)

- Matt hopes _____ poor children. (**teach**)

- Joe will go to Paris _____ art. (**study**)

Unit 12
Preposition

Then, he ran **out of** the store and down the stairs.
First, Lupin stole a diamond necklace **from** the mall.
After that, he climbed **up** the tall tree.
Finally, he jumped **over** the river to the park.

1. First, Lupin stole a diamond necklace from the mall.

2.

3.

4.

전치사 – 시간 표현 I

at + │ 시간 │ 8 o'clock │ noon │ 3:45

on + │ 날짜, 요일 │ Monday │ 21 March │ Christmas

in + │ 달, 년, 계절 │ June │ 2011 │ winter

- The mall closes **at 9:00**. • I'll see you **on Friday**. • My brother was born **in 2002**.

Circle the right words.

1 (at / on / (in)) July

2 (at / on / in) Tuesday

3 (at / on / in) spring

4 (at / on / in) 10:29

5 (at / on / in) 2009

6 (at / on / in) New year's day

7 (at / on / in) 23 October

8 (at / on / in) 5 o'clock

9 (at / on / in) night

10 (at / on / in) September

POINT 2

전치사 – 시간 표현 II

- **Before the game**, we are nervous.   ⇒ before + 명사 (~전에)
- **During the game**, we are excited.   ⇒ during + 명사 (~하는 동안)
- **After the game**, we shake hands.   ⇒ after + 명사 (~후에)
- We played **for two hours**.   ⇒ for + 시간 (~동안 : 기간)

(~~during two hours~~)

Circle the right words.

1 My brother watches football ((for) / during) three hours.

2 I wash my hands (before / after) I get back home.

3 We can't talk (for / during) the concert.

4 Halloween Day comes (before / after) Christmas.

POiNT 3 전치사 – 위치 표현

- My teacher is **next to** the bus. ➡ (～옆에)
- Tina is **between** Dave and Jake. ➡ (～사이에)
- The dog is **in front of** children. ➡ (～ 앞에)
- Jake is **behind** the dog. ➡ (～뒤에)

Look at the picture and circle the right words.

1 Dad is (**behind** / in front of) Mary.

2 Joe is (behind / between) Mary and Jenny.

3 Joe is (next to / in front of) Mom.

4 Sam is (next to / in front of) Mary.

5 Children are (behind / in front of) Parents.

6 The parents are (behind / in front of) the children.

POiNT 4 전치사 – 움직임 표현

| to : ～에게 | up : ～위를 향해 | into : ～안을 향해 |
| from : ～ 으로부터 | down : ～아래를 향해 | out of : ～밖을 향해 |

- A cat goes **to** Alice **from** Tim.
- The cat goes **up** the stairs and **down** the stairs.
- The cat goes **into** the cage and **out of** the cage.

Circle the right words.

1 Children jumped (to / **into**) the lake and swam.

2 Mike can't go (up / down) to the top of the mountain.

3 The old man got (into / out of) the house and got (into / out of) the car.

4 We walked (from / to) hotel to the bus stop.

flYing

practice for comprehension

A. Look at Sherri's diary for last week. Complete the sentence with the words from the box.

Monday	Tuesday	Thursday	Friday
12:00 Meet Sam	10:00 Swimming 11:00 Lunch	8:00~10:00 Play Piano	13:00 Piano Lesson 15:00 Party

① Sherry met Sam on Monday __at__ 12:00.

② Sherry went swimming at 10:00 _____ lunch.

③ Sherry played the piano _____ two hours on Thursday.

④ Sherry had a piano lesson _____ Friday.

⑤ _____ the piano lesson, she had a party.

at on for before after

B. Complete the sentences using the words given.

① (**next to**)

➡ The school is next to John's office.

② (**between**)

➡ The fire station is _____.

③ (**in front of**)

➡ The white car is _____.

④ (**behind**)

➡ The hotel is _____.

C. Correct the underlined mistakes, and rewrite the sentence.

1

A : Did you see Alex?

B : Yes, he walked ~~into~~ the school.

➡ Yes, he walked out of the school.

2

A : Where does the train go?

B : The train goes ~~from~~ Busan.

➡ _____

3

Maggie jumped ~~out of~~ the pool.

➡ _____

4

I watched the movie ~~during~~ 3 hours.

➡ _____

D. Look at Amy's daily schedule and write your own daily schedule.

22:00~06:30 Sleep	8:00~16:00 School	15:00~16:00 Homework	16:00~20:00 Sports Activities

Amy's Daily Schedule

Amy gets up at 6:30 in the morning.

She studies at school for 8 hours.

After school, she does her homework.

Amy does her sports activities for 4 hours.

My Daily Schedule

_____

_____

_____

_____

눈이 즐겁고, 손이 즐겁고, 머리가 즐거운

Early
GRAMMAR
A bridge between forms and functions in English Grammar

2

English!

Answer Key

눈이 즐겁고, 손이 즐겁고, 머리가 즐거운

Early
GRAMMAR
2

English!

Answer Key

woongjin
compass

p.7 She met Mr. Darling. → They got married. → They have three kids.

해석 Darling 부인은 음악 학교를 졸업했다. → 그녀는 Darling 씨를 만났다.
→ 그들은 결혼했다. → 그들은 세 명의 아이를 두었다.

p.8 POiNT ❶

2 cleaned **3** stayed **4** works

p.8 POiNT ❷

2 mopped **3** tried **4** stopped **5** planned **6** studied

p.9 POiNT ❸

Walking **1** bought **2** thought **3** went **4** had **5** spoke **6** took **7** knew **8** put

Running **2** ate **3** made

p.10 **Flying** Ⓐ **1** got
  2 had
  3 went
  4 bought
  5 left
Ⓑ **2** I ate three apples
  3 My brother studied hard
  4 I bought a new book
Ⓒ **2** go → went
  3 helps → helped
  4 gives → gave
Ⓓ Jason's week
  played soccer, went shopping, swam, helped mother
  [예시] My week
    I went to school last Monday.
    I went swimming last Wednesday.
    I watched a movie on TV last Friday.

해석 Jason의 한 주
Jason은 지난 월요일에 수학 공부를 했습니다. 그는 지난 수요일에 축구를 했습니다. 그는 지난 금요일에 쇼핑을
했습니다. Jason은 지난 주말에 수영을 했고 엄마를 도와 드렸습니다.

p.13 carrots, tomatoes

해석 Man : 지난 밤에 Sally가 요리했니?

Boy : 네. 그녀는 야채 스프를 만들었어요. 그녀는 당근과 토마토를 넣고 소금은 넣지 않았어요!

p.14 POiNT ❶

Walking **2** didn't make **3** went **4** didn't buy

Running **2** didn't work **3** didn't go **4** didn't have **5** didn't study

p.15 POiNT ❷

Walking **2** Did, clean **3** Did, have **4** Did, stop

Running **2** Did you have a great holiday?

3 Did you finish the homework?

4 Did you have a lot of homework last night?

p.16 **Flying** Ⓐ **2** ate, didn't eat

3 studied, didn't study

4 played, didn't play

Ⓑ **2** didn't have **3** stayed **4** closed

Ⓒ **2** goes → went

3 looked → look

4 did → didn't

해석 지난 월요일, Sam은 열쇠를 잃어버렸습니다. Sam은 집에 들어갈 수 없었습니다. 그래서 그는 열쇠를 찾으러 학교로 돌아갔습니다. Sam의 친구 Tom이 그와 함께 갔습니다. "네 가방을 주의 깊게 보았니?" Tom이 물었습니다. "아니. 그러지 않았어." Sam이 말했습니다.

"난 그것을 잃어버리지 않았더라. 내 뒷주머니에서 찾았어."

Words lose [lu:z] ~을 잃다, 분실하다 (– lost – lost)   key [ki:] 열쇠   carefully [kéərfəli] 주의 깊게
back pocket 뒷주머니

Ⓓ **2** Did you play soccer last year?

– [예시] Sam played / didn't play soccer last year.

3 Did you travel abroad last year?

– [예시] Sam traveled / didn't travel abroad last year.

4 Did you study English last year?

– [예시] Sam studied / didn't study English last year.

3

p.19 Dave : I'll tap dance.   Jake : I'll do magic tricks.   Tina : I'll played the guitar and sing.

해석 다음 달에 장기 자랑이 있습니다. Tina가 말했습니다. "나는 기타 치고 노래를 할 거야." Jake가 말했습니다. "나는 마술을 할 거야." Dave가 말했습니다. "나는 탭 댄스를 출 거야!" 그들은 열심히 연습할 겁니다. 그들은 재미있을 겁니다.

Words talent contest 장기 자랑   magic [mǽdʒik] 마술   trick [trík] 비법   tap dance 탭댄스를 추다
practice [prǽktis] 연습하다

p.20 POiNT ❶

2 will show **3** will be

p.20 POiNT ❷

2 is going to **3** are going to **4** am going to

p.21 POiNT ❸

Walking **2** Will **3** Will **4** Will

Running **2** No, will not(won't) **3** Yes, will

p.22 **Flying** Ⓐ **2** I'm going to walk **3** I'm going to watch **4** I'm going to drink
Ⓑ **2** Will, travel, No, will not(won't) travel, will travel
3 Will, study, No, will not(won't) study, will study
Ⓒ **2** helping → help **3** am → be **4** invented → invent

해석 우리 형 Jack은 용감합니다. 그는 경찰관이 될 것입니다. 그는 많은 사람들을 도울 것입니다.
나는 용감하지는 않지만 아주 똑똑합니다. 나는 과학자가 될 것입니다. 나는 새 로봇을 발명할 것입니다.
그 로봇은 많은 사람들을 도울 것입니다.

Words brave [breiv] 용감한   policeman [pəlí:smən] 경찰관   scientist [sáiəntist] 과학자
invent [invént] 발명하다   robot [róubət] 로봇

Ⓓ will meet, will go, will travel, will go, will be

해석 Amy가 어제 서울을 떠났다.
내일, 그녀는 대전에 있을 겁니다. 그녀는 거기에서 친구를 만날 겁니다. 다음 주에 Amy는 부산으로 갈 겁니다. 그녀는 KTX를 타고 여행을 할 겁니다. 그런 후에, 그녀는 제주도에 갈 겁니다. 여행 끝에 그녀는 아주 피곤할 겁니다.

Words leave [li:v] 떠나다 (– left – left)   end [end] 끝   trip [trip] 여행

p.25   **1** is wearing, False   **2** is carrying, False   **3** are having, True

p.26   POINT **1**

2 cook, aren't cooking

p.26   POINT **2**

1 dancing   **2** thinking   **3** going
4 having   **5** speaking   **6** taking   **7** knowing
8 putting   **9** meeting   **10** swimming

p.27   POINT **3**

Walking   **2** Is she drawing a bird?
3 Is David running very fast?
4 Are we listening to music?

Running   **2** Is, washing – No, she isn't.
3 Are, eating – Yes, I am.
4 Are, working – No, I'm not.

p.28   **Flying**   Ⓐ   **2** are, playing
3 isn't walking
4 is drinking
Ⓑ   **1** Emma is washing her face.
2 The teachers are having a tea time.
3 He is not listening to his mother.
4 They are selling strawberry candies.
Ⓒ   **2** ~~doesn't~~ → Anna isn't speaking on the phone.
3 ~~speaks~~ → Look at Sandra! She is speaking Japanese now.
4 ~~have~~ → My little brother is having some chicken in the shop.
Ⓓ   **2** She is drinking water.
3 They are running on the treadmill.
4 They are doing push-ups.

p.31

1 (can ride, climb)

2 (eats)

3 (has to get up)

4 (has to make)

5 (has to run)

(시계 반대 방향으로) 1 – 2 – 5 – 4 – 3

해석　　1. 그는 말을 타거나 암벽을 등반할 수 있습니다.

2. 그는 아침밥을 먹습니다.

3. 그는 아침에 일찍 일어나야 합니다.

4. 그는 잠자리를 정리해야 합니다.

5. 그는 2킬로미터를 뛰어야 합니다.

Words　　ride [raid] ~을 타다　　climb [klaim] 오르다　　make a bed 잠자리를 정리하다

p.32　**POiNT ❶**

2 can't　**3** can't　**4** can't

p.32　**POiNT ❷**

2 can　**3** can't

p.33　**POiNT ❸**

Walking　**2** doesn't have to　**3** doesn't have to　**4** have to

Running　**2** has to clean　**3** have to eat　**4** have to go

p.34　**Flying**　Ⓐ　**2** Can you ski? – I can/can't ski.

3 Can you ride a bike? – I can/can't ride a bike.

4 Can you drive a car? – I can/can't drive a car.

Ⓑ　**2** don't have to go

3 have to leave

4 have to wear

Ⓒ　**2** ~~have~~ → He has to work.

3 ~~can have to~~ → He has to get up at 6 o'clock.

Ⓓ　**2** have to

3 can

4 have to

p.37 2

해석   Amy, 너 아파 보여. 무슨 일이야? – 아파. 냉장고에 있던 우유를 마셨는데 냄새가 안좋았어.

Words   taste [teist] 맛을 보다. 맛이 나다   fridge [fridʒ] 냉장고   smell [smel] 냄새 맡다. 냄새 나다

p.38 POINT ①

Walking   2 sounds   3 tastes   4 smells

Running   1 soft, terrible ... (Answers can vary.)
              2 delicious, salty, terrible ... (Answers can vary.)
              3 soft, beautiful ... (Answers can vary.)
              4 soft, hard, terrible ... (Answers can vary.)
              5 small, big, beautiful, ugly ... (Answers can vary.)

p.39 POINT ②

Walking   2 slowly   3 sweet   4 happily

Running   2 behaves   3 feel   4 play

p.40 **Flying**

Ⓐ   2 The yellow cloth felt soft.
     3 The sky was black.
     4 My dad drives very fast.

Ⓑ   2 warmly
     3 bad
     4 serious

Ⓒ   2 ~~sadly~~ → The kids look sad.
     3 ~~slow~~ → The farmers work slowly.
     4 ~~wonderfully~~ → This wine tastes wonderful.

Ⓓ   tasted wonderful, looked scary, felt soft

해석   쇼핑하는 날
어제, 나는 친구들과 함께 쇼핑몰에 갔습니다. 거기에는 밴드가 있었습니다 그들은 락 음악을 연주했습니다. 그것은 훌륭하게 들렸습니다. 우리는 국수 식당에서 먹었습니다. 국수는 맛이 좋았습니다. 우리는 애완동물 가게에 갔습니다. 거기에는 뱀이 있었습니다. 무서워 보였습니다. 그리고 우리는 장난감 가게에 갔습니다. 나는 여동생을 위해 돼지 인형을 샀습니다. 아주 부드러운 느낌이었습니다.

Words   band [bænd] 음악대, 밴드   noodle [núːdl] 국수   pet [pet] 애완동물   snake [sneik] 뱀
scary [skéəri] 무서운   toy [tɔi] 인형   soft [sɔːft] 부드러운

p.43   Tom – some wheat flour, a few apples, a lot of milk

David – a lot of vegetables, a little mayonnaise

해석   Tom : 나는 사과 파이를 만들 거예요. 밀가루하고 사과 몇 개를 주세요. 우유도 많이 필요해요.

Kevin : 나는 떡을 만들고 싶어요. 쌀과 꿀을 조금 주세요. 물도 필요해요.

David : 나는 샐러드를 만들고 싶어요. 많은 야채하고 마요네즈가 좀 필요해요.

Words   wheat [*h*wíːt] 밀   flour [fláuər] 밀가루   mayonnaise [méiənéiz] 마요네즈

p.44   POiNT **1**

Walking **2** There aren't any flowers in the vase.

3 There are some apples on the table.

4 We have some pizza for you.

Running **2** some **3** any **4** some, any

p.45   POiNT **2**

2 many **3** much **4** many **5** much **6** many

p.45   POiNT **3**

2 a little **3** a little **4** a few **5** a little **6** a few

p.46 **Flying** **A** **2** some flowers

3 any bread

B **2** many books

3 many students

C **2** a little bread

3 a few minutes

D **2** much

3 a few

4 any

E • a little bread or a lot of bread

• a few socks, a lot of socks or many socks

• a few batteries or a lot of batteries

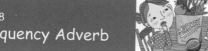
p.49   **1** Tony, Sandra

         2 tofu and vegetables

해석   Sandra : 나는 대개 두부와 야채를 많이 먹어요. 나는 결코 햄버거는 안 먹어요!

           Tony : 나는 자주 햄버거를 먹어요. 항상 좋아할 겁니다!

p.50   POiNT **1**

     2 well   **3** carefully   **4** loudly

     5 very   **6** slowly   **7** hard

p.50   POiNT **2**

     [예시] **1** never   **2** sometimes   **3** often

           4 sometimes   **5** always   **6** never

p.51   POiNT **3**

Walking   **2** I usually finish my homework in the morning.

           3 Mike doesn't always work on weekends.

           4 I will never forget your help.

Running   **2** Sam never studies hard.

           3 Sam is sometimes busy.

           4 Sam always goes fishing.

p.52   **Flying**   Ⓐ   **2** I can never remember his birthday.

                 3 I don't often eat fast food.

                 4 The train isn't usually late.

          Ⓑ   **2** can never forget

                 3 doesn't often rain

                 4 are never at home

          Ⓒ   Sunday is never a quiet day for our family.

             He always works hard.

             Dad is usually busy cutting grass.

             I must always help mom and dad.

해석   우리 가족들에게 일요일은 결코 조용한 날이 아닙니다. 우리는 엄마를 도와야 합니다. 밖에서 남동생, Chris는 창문을 닦습니다. 그는 항상 열심히 일합니다. 정원에서는 아빠가 대개 잔디를 깎으십니다. 나는 집안일을 싫어하지만 항상 엄마, 아빠를 도와야 합니다.

　quiet [kwáiət] 조용한　　outside [áutsáid] 바깥쪽, 외부　　grass [græs] 풀, 잔디
chore [tʃɔːr] (집안) 자질구레한 일

Ⓓ　[예시]　My mom always water the plants on Sundays.
　　　My sister sometimes wash the dishes.
　　　My little brother often cleans the window.

p.55　　**1** False　**2** True　**3** True　**4** False

Words　　weight [weit] 무게, 체중　　height [hait] 키　　Tusk [tʌsk] (코끼리의) 엄니　　skin [skin] 가죽, 피부

p.56　　POiNT **1**

2 faster　**3** earlier　**4** higher　**5** happier　**6** hotter

p.56　　POiNT **2**

2 easier than　**3** younger than　**4** more beautiful than

p.57　　POiNT **3**

Walking　**2** the youngest, the oldest
　　　　　3 the lowest, the highest
　　　　　4 the cheapest, the most expensive

Running　**2** better, the best
　　　　　3 colder, the coldest
　　　　　4 harder, the hardest

p.58　　**Flying**　　Ⓐ　**2** older than, the oldest
　　　　　　　　　　3 taller than, the tallest
　　　　　　　　　　4 cheaper than, the cheapest
　　　　　　　　Ⓑ　**2** The sun is hotter than the moon.
　　　　　　　　　　3 A sheep is slower than a horse.
　　　　　　　　　　4 An elephant's ear is bigger than a rabbit's ear.
　　　　　　　　Ⓒ　**2** ~~more fast~~ → Driving a car is faster than riding a bike.
　　　　　　　　　　3 ~~more pretty~~ → Yours is prettier.
　　　　　　　　　　4 ~~dry~~ → Sahara is a drier place than Seoul.
　　　　　　　　Ⓓ　[예시] The panda lives in China.
　　　　　　　　　　　　　The polar bear lives in the Arctic.
　　　　　　　　　　　　　The panda is friendlier than the polar bear.
　　　　　　　　　　　　　The panda is cuter than the polar bear.
　　　　　　　　　　　　　The polar bear is faster than the panda.
　　　　　　　　　　　　　The polar bear is bigger than the panda.

Words　　the Arctic 북극　　cute [kjuːt] 귀여운 (– cuter – cutest)
　　　　　friendly [fréndli] 친구다운, 친절한 (– friendlier – friendliest)

p.61 cooking food, swimming, going camping

해석 John : 스케이트보드 타기가 내가 제일 좋아하는 스포츠야. 요리하기는 재미없어.

Lisa : 난 수영하기가 재미없어. 내가 좋아하는 활동은 캠핑가는 거야.

p.62 POiNT ❶

Walking **2** Eating – ⓐ
3 climbing – ⓒ
4 knitting – ⓑ

Running **2** Ice skating – 주어 → 아이스 스케이트 타는 것은 아주 어렵다.
3 Cooking – 주어 → 요리하는 것은 재미있다.
4 collecting – 보어 → 나의 취미는 오래된 동전을 모으는 것이다.

p.63 POiNT ❷

Walking **2** enjoys – (playing)
3 kept – (telling)
4 finished – (making)
5 stopped – (smoking)

Running **2** doing **3** using **4** watching **5** swimming **6** driving

p.64 **Flying** Ⓐ **2** enjoy
3 mind
4 keep
Ⓑ **2** cooking Korean food
3 Living in the city
4 helping other people
Ⓒ **2** Driving is faster than taking a bus.
3 My grandmom enjoys getting up early in the morning.
4 Eating fast food is not good for your health.
Ⓓ [예시] hobby, listening to music, swimming, eating *gimbap*

해석 Rona가 가장 좋아하는 취미는 이야기를 읽는 것입니다. 그녀는 축구하기도 좋아합니다. Rona는 피자 먹는 것도
좋아합니다.

p.67   **1** to become **2** taking care of

해석   Kevin : 난 선생님이 되고 싶어. 작은 아이들 가르치는 것을 좋아해.

Sam : 난 수의사가 되고 싶어. 동물들 돌보는 것을 좋아해.

Words   vet [vet] 수의사   take care of ~을 돌보다

p.68   POiNT **1**

2 learns, (to play) → Maria는 테니스 하는 것을 배운다.
3 decided, (to buy) → 엄마는 새 컴퓨터를 사기로 결정했다.
4 need, (to go) → 늦었어. 우리는 집에 가야 해.
5 hope, (to go) → 나는 내년에 해외에 나가기를 바란다.

p.68   POiNT **2**

2 to study, studying
3 to go
4 to work, working
5 to watch, watching
6 to walk, walking

p.69   POiNT **3**

2 to open – 형용사 → 나는 문을 열 열쇠가 없다.
3 to meet – 명사 → Jane은 그녀의 사촌을 만나기를 바란다.

p.69   POiNT **4**

2 to jog
3 to buy a shirt

p.70   **Flying**   Ⓐ **2** to do, to visit
3 doing, to watch
4 to ask, to meet
Ⓑ **2** to bake
3 to cut
4 to sit on
Ⓒ **2** I want to see you soon.
3 We hope to visit your country next summer.
4 Would you like to go to the park?

D to become, to become, to teach, to study

해석   Sam은 의사가 되기로 결심했습니다. 그는 아프리카에 가서 어린이들을 도울 겁니다.

Lisa는 무용수가 되려고 열심히 합니다. 그녀는 많이 유명해지기를 원합니다.

Matt는 가난한 어린이들을 가르치고 싶습니다. 그는 선생님이 되려고 열심히 공부합니다.

Joe는 4년 전에 그림을 시작했습니다. 그는 미술 공부를 하려고 파리에 갈 계획입니다.

Words   decide [disáid] 결심하다   become [bikʌ́m] ~이 되다   famous [féiməs] 유명한
plan [plæn] ~을 계획하다   art [ɑːrt] 예술

p.73 **2** Then, he ran out of the store and down the stairs.

3 After that, he climbed up the tall tree.

4 Finally, he jumped over the river to the park.

해석   첫째, 루팡은 상점가에서 다이아몬드 목걸이를 훔쳤다.

그리고, 그는 가게를 빠져 나와 계단을 내려왔다.

그리고 나서, 그는 키 큰 나무 위에 올라서 사라졌다.

마지막으로, 그는 강을 건너 공원으로 갔다.

Words   steal [stiːl] ~을 훔치다 (– stole – stolen)   necklace [néklis] 목걸이   stair [stɛər] 계단

river [rívər] 강

p.74   POINT **1**

2 on **3** in **4** at **5** in **6** on

7 on **8** at **9** at **10** in

p.74   POINT **2**

2 after **3** during **4** before

p.75   POINT **3**

2 between **3** in front of **4** next to **5** in front of **6** behind

p.75   POINT **4**

2 up **3** out of, into **4** from

p.76   **Flying**   **A**   **2** before

3 for

4 on

5 After

B   **2** between the factory and the gas station

3 in front of the police station

4 behind the bank

C   **2** The train goes to Busan.

3 Maggie jumped into the pool.

4 I watched the movie for 3 hours.

D   [예시] My daily schedule

I get up at 8:00 in the morning.

15

I studies at school for 6 hours.

After school, I play with my friends.

I take a piano lesson for 1 hour.

해석   Amy의 스케줄

Amy는 아침에 6시 30분에 일어납니다. 그녀는 학교에서 8시간 동안 공부합니다. 방과 후, 그녀는 숙제를 합니다. Amy는 스포츠 활동을 4시간 동안 합니다.

Words   get up 일어나다   after school 방과 후   activity [æktívəti] 활동

눈이 즐겁고, 손이 즐겁고, 머리가 즐거운

Early
GRAMMAR
2

English!

- ➡ 언어의 형태(form)와 실질적 의미(meaning),
  그리고 활용(use)까지 고루 학습
- ➡ 탄탄한 기본기로 학교 문법 완벽 대비
- ➡ 내신 및 각종 인증 시험 적응 훈련 가능

⭐ (주)컴퍼스미디어